# PEOPLE WASTE

## The Antithesis of Quality Leadership

Doug Booker

Copyright © 2016 Doug Booker

All rights reserved.

ISBN-10: 1535564253
ISBN-13: 978-1535564250

**PEOPLE WASTE -** The Antithesis of Quality Leadership

*"Please know I realize I have borrowed and used pics, quotes & graphics from a variety of sources. I have attempted to give credit. In some cases I do not know. Where I knew who, I have given credit."* D. Booker

# **TABLE OF CONTENTS**

|    | Acknowledgments         | I       |
|----|-------------------------|---------|
|    | A Short Story           | pg. 8   |
| 1  | Intro / Purpose         | pg. 16  |
| 2  | What's Waste            | pg. 33  |
| 3  | RVP(s)                  | pg. 50  |
| 4  | ID Your Sphere          | pg. 55  |
| 5  | Process Planning        | pg. 68  |
| 6  | Visioning Success       | Pg. 76  |
| 7  | Assess Your Sphere      | pg. 86  |
| 8  | Your Other RVPs         | pg. 93  |
| 9  | Making it Happen        | pg. 101 |
| 10 | Wrapping Up             | pg. 107 |
|    | Supplemental References | pg. 113 |
|    | Author / Previous books | pg. 115 |

## DEDICATION / ACKNOWLEDGMENTS

Thanks to all those who have allowed me into their 'Leadership Learning' world. To learn with, from and through their struggles.

Thanks to the Leaders who grow, improve and build rather than maintain the status quo.

For the leaders I have taught, grown and learned with; thanks for helping me learn the lessons of Leadership and Relationships within these pages, to share with others.

Thanks to all who have trusted me with themselves, their careers, their growth and their people.

Douglas M. Booker

## ***A LITTLE STORY...***

*Bob is VP of Product Design & Development for a medium size Injection Molding/Mfg Company – IMMC Inc.*

*With coffee in hand, he is pouring over Monday morning weekend-recovery issues, catching up on emails and rethinking weekly planning/calendar items. He struggles to focus due to an impending major deal for the company, as well as the ongoing company-wide process integration change. The integration piece must be completed before the deal can really be completed. Two weeks, yikes! Bob ponders and mutters to himself as he firmly shuts his door spilling a bit of coffee returning to his desk. Jackie, his Exec Assistant observes and goes to ask Jeff why the boss is obviously upset about something.*

*"...Crud, I guess my week is screwed again. Golf game with vendors, nope; performance talks with Becky and Bill, nope; work on the new workflow idea, nope; and scratch helping HR with the new hire orientations for the third time! I have got to regain control of my*

*schedule and calendar, dang it. Jerked around, fire-fighting again and I'm supposed to be one of the few here running the joint! More people stuff wasting my time because of their issues with each other... That's all this is about... Dumb, just dumb.*

*I know the 'deal' and integration completion are both going to be another last minute, midnight hour fire drill. We should've been so much further down the road with all this by now. The CEO has no clue, I gotta fill him in but he's going to go off on Mike and Rick if I do. Of course they need him to light a fire under their butts; but they'll be royally PO'd at me knowing I was the one firing him up. They will obviously know I got them dumped on... Rick, what a jerk really.*

*I gotta figure a way to connect or fix those two, get them talking without the boss coming down on them. Only ten workdays left and really, for the most part things aren't too bad, most is seemingly on track. Still we should have been at this point about two weeks back... Really three!*

*Jeff is solid as the point-man project manager and despite some issues with his team's lack of teamwork and being down one headcount - Jeff will make it happen I think. I really need to get a sense of where he is exactly although he so hates to be watched/checked on.... He takes it so personally, like I don't trust him. I will catch him after the Ops Update briefing this afternoon and pick his brain a bit. Maybe I could get Jackie to slide back there and see what she could find out...*

*I better drop by Sara's cube today some time, or at least by tomorrow morning to see if she and Jeff are in synch with everything. If she doesn't give me a warm and fuzzy on their progress, I gotta get Rick involved. Jeff isn't the easiest guy to work with, but she's the real issue here. Rick just needs to exert some leadership over her, quit accepting excuses and hold her accountable. Guess we could all do some better 'accountability stuff' with our folks.*

*Dangit, but those two and their running issues and conflicts definitely worries me. Jeff and Sara are the classic personality conflict - each is so valuable and just so key here. If we could get them on the same page, they could be such a dynamic duo. They are just such strong A-type personalities.*

*I wonder why I haven't heard something back from Bill on the vendor questions with integration-completion. He's such a procrastinator anyway and on top of that I know he's still bitter about not getting his guy that Senior Director Ops Management job back first of the year. I know he still thinks Mike and I didn't support him. He's probably just sitting over there not communicating because he knows it's worrying me ...so petty, what a pain in the butt.*

*If I could just drag the five of them into a room - maybe I could at least get them all on the same page to pull this off by end of the month. Maybe, maybe not. Might make it worse though, damn. Actually I got no choice, I have to; after lunch I will get Jackie in here to think this through and see if the two of us can figure out how to make us all function as a freakin' team at least through this project. She is good with this stuff with such a good relationship with Jeff and Bill which could help pull this off. What would I do without her...?*

*Jackie can almost always do her magic in working around personalities and stuff. It seems she has no enemies and is really just rock solid with all people around the entire market. Likely something there she could teach us all, which we could all learn from I'm sure...*

*We gotta do some team-building next quarter, this crap is killing us.*

*OK, onto other items. On no, well crud. I forgot completely I promised to help facilitate that Culture session this afternoon with Bill. Like we don't have enough on our plate without taking on new culture initiatives. I put him off twice before. I gotta bump this other stuff to tomorrow I guess, which means we would only really have nine days to go? I can't do that, it's gotta get done today or we won't pull this off. Gotta call Bill and see if Culture can wait...*

*I know the boss is dying to know how if we are moving forward on the Integration procedures NLT tomorrow. That one would be done if it wasn't for everyone's pain in the butt Murray, what a nightmare. Beth isn't helping either as she badgers him relentless about missed deadlines and his Warehouse manager. Man, if freaking people would just get along and get on the same page.*

*First of the month I am getting the boss to take the whole gang out for a drink and see if we can make some headway with our 'teamwork' and relations. It is killing us and I know the boss is*

**PEOPLE WASTE** - The Antithesis of Quality Leadership

*irritated by our lack of communications. Why can't we just get along? Of course the boss doesn't help anything not fixing the Mike n' Rick conflict going on a couple years now; hurting us all big time all over the organization...*

*Of course if we don't pull off these initiatives he ain't taking us anywhere except maybe to the unemployment line.*

*Getting stuff done just shouldn't be this hard. What a waste. We could be so much more..."*

*Jackie turns out to be the hero, schmoozing through the conflicts and personalities for us once again. The integration and sale both get done, yes at the midnight hour. There was just so much wasted time all related to people stuff – conflicts, personalities, communicating barriers, conversations put off, disagreements, procrastination, him not liking her, her not appreciating him, etc etc etc. Dumb stuff. If not for our dysfunctional people-system, all could have been done by mid-month undoubtedly!*

*What are your thoughts right now considering this story and our title, 'People Waste'?*

## **JOURNALING - THOUGHTS GOING ON IN YOUR HEAD:**

- Throughout your new 'handbook' here there is space provided for capturing your thoughts. Did you think you were just going to sit there and read? ☺

**PEOPLE WASTE -** The Antithesis of Quality Leadership

# 1

# INTRO / PURPOSE

*'Insanity is doing the same thing over and over and over again …and expecting different results.'*
Albert Einstein

This was nearly titled 'TIME WASTERS' but for the fear of being perceived as just another book on time-management. The little clocks throughout hopefully will do that job of keeping the reader focused on the time-killer dynamic that PEOPLE WASTE does indeed speak to within these pages.

I want to clearly state there are three core concepts intertwined throughout the book. Each is here for two distinct audiences – 1) the Leader in pursuit of continued learning, self-development and growth, and 2) the organization overall and management at the top - to lead the way in changing the culture.

These three big picture concepts are:

- ✓ **People Waste** – defining and 'seeing' the cost of people dysfunction, relational issues, baggage, avoided but necessary conversation and communication barriers in general.

**PEOPLE WASTE -** The Antithesis of Quality Leadership

- ✓ **The Leadership Sphere** – awareness of the need to intentionally manage relationships throughout our sphere; <u>all</u> 360 degrees and with <u>all</u>! This is presented here through the introduction of a new term, Relational Value Points (RVP).

- ✓ **Vision Achievement** – the challenge of visioning; a template/strategy for managing our sphere toward vision-realization. A challenging vision requires intentionally-managed leadership.

This may at this point seem theoretical. This is not the case. This is not about theory but about absolutely practical application.

This book's targeted audience is indeed leaders and leadership. It is especially appropriate for any medium to large sized organization. Corporate America for sure, but any sizeable organization (business or not) – this fits! It is furthermore focused in many ways, upon the senior level leader (as mentioned above). Still it is extremely relevant to each and every key player in the organization. We will place our emphasis here on the leader because when the leader changes, so do their people, teams and spheres. The multiplier-dynamic of 'leadership' is why we should and must address leaders first in these regards.

Consider this: Leaders tend to lead utilizing one of these two components primarily – RELATIONSHIP (being liked, personality, caring for, team-player, friendship, etc) or

ACCOUNTABILITY (holding people's feet to the fire, deadlines, micro-managing, perfectionism, no mistakes, directing, etc). Neither really works well in a vacuum which is the root cause relationships suffer and struggle. If I am about RELATIONSHIP (liking & being liked), I let you get away with things, lessen standards, or minimally not hold you accountable. If you hold me accountable, you must not be my friend?!?! If I am about ACCOUNTABILITY, I likely don't seem likeable, mission first and foremost; and therefore come across as a hard-case nobody likes with few friends.

Ideally of course, the true leader balances both in practice. He/she practices both by being highly relational while also holding people accountable. Most believe you can't be both.

The real leader is the one who has come to understand that 'yes, I can be both' and it works amazingly well. Somewhere in the midst of NOT balancing these two components is where the functionality and communications between any two people breaks down. This is true for all people throughout the workplace. Again for our purposes here, we are dwelling on the Leader's leadership (of his followers/subordinates) in these regards.

**PEOPLE WASTE -** The Antithesis of Quality Leadership

The practicality of what is between the covers of this book in regard to relations in the workplace will grab you immediately. This I am sure because,

- You, the leader 'felt' the story up above as situations and scenarios you deal with and that you see in your sphere of players around you.

- You, the leader 'resemble' and will recognize all this on coming pages; as your existence (as well as that of most in management and players in your organization).

- You, the leader will recognize the value and need in the plan put before you in this template.

- You, the leader will see the logic and practicality of how one can mechanically manage relationships to achieve personal success (as well as achieving the vision)!

- You, the leader, finally will realize the waste in how things (communications, bottlenecks, dysfunction among people, etc) really are throughout organizations. I'm betting this includes yours!

Here's the bottom line. What *should be* such tremendous assets to your organization: LEADERSHIP, RELATIONS, and PEOPLE - are not being 'all they should be' to your organization. There is huge waste going on within what most refer to as 'your most valuable resource'!

You are likely thinking, '...Booker maybe we're not great in these areas. But really, Leadership and People-stuff is costing us?'

In fact the ineffectiveness of your organizational behavior/communications and more specifically your leader's behaviors/communications - could even be called wasteful. No, let me change that - NOT 'could be'. A lack of trust, transparency and relationship are huge wasters within your cubicles, offices, board rooms, and your halls!

*'How much?'* you have to be wondering, right?

Trust the Coach here (and 40 years leading and/or working with leadership and upper level management). This *'how much'* could be very significant. You can additionally trust in this whole assertion (people waste) by the simple realization of how much literature is on bookstore shelves. Volumes continue to be written about workplace dysfunction, conflict, communicating, relationships, building teams, creating trust, culture, etc. It's all there on the bookshelves because organizations (leaders!) are not fully addressing people to people exchanges, communications and organizational behavior.

## **PEOPLE WASTE** - The Antithesis of Quality Leadership

Status-Quo management, assumed leadership skills and dysfunctional behavior (between leaders, peers, internal customers and followers) is impacting your culture. This negative relational-impact on productivity and bottom line is somewhere between 30-50%! All this people-stuff which should be a multiplier for your biz is actually subtracting from it...

Just so you don't miss out on what was just said, that is 30-50% of what should be your most valuable resource is being wasted! And the time wasted is astounding if you are indeed open to all this and willing to accept what you know is going on all around you, ...all around you and your sphere, ...all around every other organizational leader and his/her sphere as well. That's a lot of 'all around' wastefulness.

Right! Your 'PEOPLE SYSTEM' is costing you likely, let's just assume something between that 30-50%. Let's low-ball this and go with 30%.

What we are really honing in on and targeting here in this book is the *leader's relationship* piece in all this. I actually believe ONLY the best-of-the-best companies are the ONLY ones ONLY wasting 30%. If you are the average company, you are likely averaging something closer to losing 40% of your people potential!

You are likely resisting this notion a bit here, trying to not believe this. You would be in the majority my friend!

You might be wanting to bust out with a big ol "...where's the proof Booker?"

> NOTE: *For the first time, let me tell you I am not here to prove something to you (that you already know is true). I am going to place a few links in the back of the book for those who may want to do a bit of further research. I have indeed done my research through hundreds of leaders, teams and staff interactions, trainings and consultations. I have touched and validated all this conceptually with 1000s of individual players in organizations (and students in academic institutions where I have taught). The numbers and percentages could be challenged and if you wish to, go ahead, feel free... Prove me wrong – no, don't go wasting your time even more!*

<u>Now back to our conversation.</u>

...For if you were to accept all this as the leader, this would imply this is about you. Your responsibility. Your fault. Yours to fix! Yikes.

This is the numbness that exists within each of us and within our workplaces, society and corporate cultures. We have come to accept a mindset and thinking of (or like)...

- less than 'good' relationships,
- dysfunctional teams,

**PEOPLE WASTE -** The Antithesis of Quality Leadership

- it's no big deal,
- hard to find good people these days,
- poor people behavior is just how it is,
- that synergy-thing (which conceptually takes us past the 100% mark), as just being hypothetical stuff to discuss over coffee, and….
- the time wasted is just part of the organizational behavioral 'norm'.

We, the workplace have become accepting of dysfunction or baggage between/among people as being …OKAY

…(or) FINE

…(or) JUST THE WAY IT IS

…(or) GOOD ENOUGH.

We are, after all, getting our 400 widgets/day produced. Never mind that the 'people waste' prevents you from producing what …maybe 520!

That's 30% waste, IF you are one of the 'best of the best'!

Decades around leaders and cultures has me convinced of the significance-factor of all this. For further validation, cause and/or reasoning - do I need to also mention the breakdown of the society and family; and oh yeah all the technological advances that drives us into smartphone screens rather than people's faces? All this and more is only gradually making this waste-factor worse and worse... Chew on that for a moment.

So here it is, short and sweet, less than 100 pages. The waste I just referenced you to is heavily about the 'relationships among leaders'. And/or the lack of relationship among leaders and key players largely near the top of organizations.

- ✓ Trust the Coach here. If you are a leader, this must right now become your Leadership Guide. This is all 'MUST DO' if you wish to stop the PEOPLE WASTE going on right now,

...in your organization,

...on your own team,

...within your own sphere of influence (leadership/relationships).

Listen, this may take a bit to spread throughout the organization. However, around YOU and within your sphere we are talking a major fix/shift in a few months!

**PEOPLE WASTE -** The Antithesis of Quality Leadership

This message and content here is for those (you) who see LEADERSHIP as its own skillset. For those who see LEADERSHIP as (your) next life's work to master. This is for those of us who are serious about growing your leadership and are willing to do the actual focused work to achieve it.

As much as there will always be to learn and add to your LEADERSHIP skillset or toolbox (for those you lead) - addressing your relationship-sphere is the foundation you first need to have in place. This is a truth! This whole sphere thing I keep mentioning, we're getting ready to get into it!

You must get and accept this 'waste' premise and buy into your responsibility (as a seasoned leader) to eliminate this waste. Begin with you, your relations and your sphere. You have mastered other stuff; now it is time to master leadership ...and your sphere. Let others continue mastering 'that' other stuff relevant to the biz. You've been there, done that. Please don't keep doing that!

This content, this template, strategy and message is indeed the foundation of LEADERSHIP-mastery. Addressing and eliminating People Waste is your job, part of this new mastery.

Once again, stop doing the work of a level or two downward and begin going and growing 'where you want to go'! Think on this one for a moment: You need to stop managing (maintaining) that current 65% relational success and begin leading and eliminating.

THINK ON THIS: Many leadership books to include my previous four (listed in the back of this book) are great resources undoubtedly. Well mine are for sure (GRINNING AT YA'). However, this concept and template should now rule and 'lead' your Leadership-Learning my friend! Begin executing this and THEN go keep-on continually improving your leadership skills as well...

## *'Never Stop Learning'*

Let me take this previous thought about your 'Leadership Learning' another step or two further for clarification.

90% of the leadership teaching out there (and likely 90% of what you have learned thus far) is 90% focused on your 'vertical' leadership dynamics.

Huh...

That 90% is about your downward (vertical) – YOU and those YOU lead. It is all 'what leadership is and how to lead those you lead'. As critical as this is to your success undoubtedly, it is only part of the picture. A big part, but still only a part. It is just a part or portion of your

**PEOPLE WASTE -** The Antithesis of Quality Leadership

Leadership-Relationship sphere.

Listen. Think. Focus here. Don't just read. ☺

Chances are you are missing out on just how much this whole sphere is impacting your productivity and success. That sphere 'is your job'. Soon, very soon, if it hasn't already begun - NOT addressing your entire relational-sphere will cause you to stumble. Continuing to merely focus on the relationship with your boss and those you lead (all your verticals) is a 'miss'.

This is again, assuming you haven't already begun to stumble and struggle unconsciously, unknowingly. It's that numbness thing, trust me. You have fallen into the trap that 'relating to most people fairly well' (those horizontals) is good enough. Is 65% good enough?

IF you (the senior leader) begin executing what is on these coming pages regarding your relationships ...you WILL BEGIN leading at a higher level! This is a focus on and about ALL of the critical people in your world, and not just some of them. It is about your entire sphere of relations (RVPs) - because all of them matter; all impact you, and all are contributing to your level of success as a leader (positively & negatively).

I call each of these people in your sphere - your 'Relational Value Points'. RVPs for short, which I will explain more about shortly.

I am betting you have never REALLY considered the people around you in such a way (and this is not about one of those anonymous one-stop workshop 360degree drills).

That's it.

Read this, understand it.

Internalize it.

Buy into it.

Commit.

Get your calendar working for you.

Keep this next to your coffee, frequent it frequently.

Have the conversations.

No kidding. No blowing off any of it (discussions & conversations). No blowing off, any of your RVPs (the people)! And yes, that's right, you can't even blow off the knuckleheads ...those horizontals you struggle with - You ol' knucklehead you. That's just your ol' knucklehead coach here messing with you, mind you☺.

**PEOPLE WASTE -** The Antithesis of Quality Leadership

Persist executing this concept for your next 3-4 months and you will be leading ...and you will be so much happier within the culture! IF done, you cannot NOT be leading ...and you will be 'continually improving' your leadership effectiveness every day, week and month thereafter! Promise.

No shortcuts. No magic pill.

Relationships must become what you believe to be 'Your Most Valuable Resource' and biggest priority!

I promise that after seeing the results of doing this I am getting ready to propose – you will always do this thereafter! And you will then not only be modeling great stuff, but you will be teaching leadership. That's LEADERSHIP success. Suddenly you will begin to realize and feel the fun of leadership!

## *"Begin with the End in Mind."*

Stephen Covey

The content of this book - what's proposed and these relational-dynamics may seem way too simplistic and obvious.

I suggest you digest it all before judging; my bet is you will be in agreement, with ALL of it. You will realize why the obvious hasn't been happening or working. I am also willing to bet you are right now falling way short of all this 'obvious' stuff!

I can assure you, in fact I promise you - this is the key, and final piece to your success as an organizational leader. It is also the key to your leadership happiness. Begin accepting this now, *'relationship strengthening is a conscious act of intentional un-ending efforts, and it is my job.'*

Very few leaders do this ...or will do this. I am hoping I am wrong, but I am fairly certain 'most' who read this won't do it. Real leaders - those you admire and that you have been thinking of in the previous pages - are to varying degrees doing these obvious things intentionally!

It all must be a matter of intentionality! Otherwise relation-mending, confrontations, conversations, accountability, resolving conflict, and/or hard talks are just too easy to blow off. Sadly this is the norm with most managers – doing little in these regards and pretending 'all is fine'. Yes, that was me challenging YOU☺!

Managers (maintainers) will find excuses for not doing

this. As you read onward, excuses will find their way into your head. <u>The Leader in you knows instinctively this would work if you did it.</u> Your insecurities will try to convince you to go on to that Ops Update meeting instead (or how about one of these),

"...It's too time consuming,

...he won't work with me,

...she's such a pain,

...I've tried before,

...nobody can work with her,

...I don't like confrontation,

...I don't know how to approach him,

...I'm right, he's wrong,

...he/she is hopeless,

...I need a haircut,

...I have way more important stuff to do..."

> Do you see how just conjuring up these kinds of excuses is wasteful (all that delaying of the inevitable / procrastinating)?  'Pay me now or pay me later' seems to apply here.  Please ponder this for a moment.

- ✓ For sure one of this book's messages is about the waste in organizations and the waste that leaders allow due to their own in-action.  It is not only about the leader's relational-wastes, but also all that waste going on with your people down below in their relationship dysfunctions with others, …partially caused by your (their boss) own relationship dysfunctions up above them!  Chew on that one.

Get it?

- ✓ <u>Your</u> dysfunctions and bottlenecks at your level frequently cause much of <u>their</u> dysfunctions and bottlenecks also!

# 2

# WHAT'S WASTE

*"The quality of a leader is reflected in the standards they set for themselves first, and then with the standards of those they lead."* Ray Kroc paraphrased a bit

For you Quality Management types - Lean, TQM, Six Sigma, etc - this book is NOT about *that* Operations kind of 'waste'.

This not about operational-processes, root-cause analysis or workflow dynamics emphasized in quality programs and efforts. It does however have amazing parallels and is of the same premise in a multitude of ways. [It is the piece left out of those efforts normally]

We are just replacing <u>operational-processes</u> with <u>people-processes</u>. We are looking at people, relationships, accountabilities and communications as a process!?!

As long as you are into that 'Quality Management' world way of thinking - let me offer these thoughts which I penned many years back:

*Our workplace (people) relationships AND our workplace operating systems both have in common what in the Quality*

*Management world is known as 'bottlenecks'. So we're on common ground, let me offer this definition for a <u>bottleneck</u>:*

*'... a point within a system where the flow and/or productivity is disrupted or slowed down which then requires problem-solving or extra effort or expending resources to address the problem to get the flow back up to where it should be. Without addressing it, (in some cases because we don't realize it) there will be waste occcuring....'*

*Now you won't find that in Webster's or your Quality Management materials — but it will suffice to get us on the same page. Here's what struck me as a 'people' perspective on these Quality Management concepts – again applied to people, relationships, leadership and teamwork.*

*Try to see or picture how teams (teamwork or working relations) could be thought of much like any other operation or process....*

*Let's call your team a PEOPLE-SYSTEM. However instead of machinery and equipment, we are speaking of people's relationships, teamwork, attitudes, knowledge, communications, things flowing, everything being in sync, etc. Each part of the operation (person or relationship) must support the next part for teamwork to occur smoothly and effectively. When this is really cooking, we might refer to it as synergy!*

*When there is a kink in the system it is a bottleneck or waste issue...*

**PEOPLE WASTE -** The Antithesis of Quality Leadership

*When people function well together, the result is a highly efficient and productive people-process in terms of meeting goals, success, productivity, happiness, effiiciency and accomplishing results. When things don't work well, it can nearly always be worked backward to some people-type of bottleneck causing the slowdown!*

*Here are some of your PEOPLE-SYSTEM bottlenecks that come to mind. Some or maybe all are inevitable from time to time, but do require our attention to resolve as quickly as possible. Think how each if it's a negative, becomes a TEAM-bottleneck…*

- ***CAPABILITY*** *(knowledge, know-how, education, training and experience to do the job)*
- ***RELATIONSHIPS*** *(open-ness, honesty, transparency, understanding and acceptance of others)*
- ***NEW PLAYERS*** *(new people to the team can't become productive and effective on the team until accepted, comfortable, trusted and relations established and the newness fear is overcome.)*
- ***PAST ISSUES*** *(problems that individuals have had with others on the team that have not been addressed…but rather carried around as baggage or grudges or minimally, being uncooperative).*
- ***ATTITUDES** / (NEGATIVISM)* *( some of us don't realize how important this overly used word is..when I carry around my attitude on my coat-sleeve…others see it and avoid us)."I'm no good at" thinking also plays in here…*
- ***COMMUNICATION*** *(when I fail to communicate openly and effectively with other team members, it affects the overall team's efficiency… this can be intentional or purely accidental).*

- **UNCLEAR ROLES / EXPECTATIONS** *(can be a failure of the organization or leaders to clarify functional areas OR that a team member sees his/her role one way and others see it another way...conflict, misunderstanding, unfairness, etc... begin to raise their ugly head).*
- **PERSONALITY – DIFFERENCES / DIVERSITY** *(it's reality— it needs to be and must be understood, studied and utilized to our advantage).*
- **ACCOUNTABILITY** *(inconsistent or lack of accountability impacting productivity and relationships)*
- **UNRESOLVED CONFLICTS / MISUNDERSTANDINGS** *(someone did or said something that you took the wrong way and you decide to hold it against them for the rest of their lives).*
- **TRUST** *(a team cannot reach peak performance and success without it...trust in each other to do their part, fulfill commitments, meet deadlines, respect feelings, opinions and thoughts)*

Organizations and teams will have these sorts of bottlenecks, that's a given. The question is 'can we as leaders spot them, take action and resolve (eliminate the waste)'? What we have to grasp is that these have a significant impact on the overall workflow (pace, productivity, quality, synergy, etc)...
...of the TEAM
...of your SPHERE
...of the BIZ!

**PEOPLE WASTE -** The Antithesis of Quality Leadership

So this is about the waste that goes on daily in the workplace. Waste(s) due to ineffective, under-developed and otherwise 'bad' 1:1 organizational communications from top to bottom.

It is about the people waste within your people-system.

This is again with a focus on the leaders (with/among other leaders & key players). However once again don't lose sight of the fact that the same stuff goes on throughout the biz with all people, no matter their role, or what seat they occupy.

Let's not move on too quickly. Ponder this,

- Think of just a couple of those dozens or maybe hundreds of 1:1 'weak or bad' bottlenecks going on throughout your organization.

- Now picture how those unresolved-bottlenecks frequently get worse and worse (over days, months and even years). This happens as people...

    - ✓ dislike one another and grow in that dislike;
    - ✓ differing opinions turning others into the enemy;
    - ✓ the avoidance of each other;
    - ✓ very slow efforts/work on new relations;

- ✓ finding shortcuts rather than deal with knucklehead;

- ✓ procrastination of communicating about important stuff, etc...

Because I don't like you ...or maybe I just don't know you yet. This is a bottleneck. That is waste until it is eliminated. See? Let me share just a bit more regarding 'what is waste'!

*Scenario: Let's take a company of 100 people, that's 100 spheres of relationships - 360degrees around each person from CEO to newest newbie.* Let's break down ONE of these spheres and list a few possible relational waste dynamics that could play out (again, in any given sphere).

- ↓ And as you read these below, please ponder their reality and when you maybe last experienced any of these. Then remember to multiply all this by 100 (spheres)! That's a lot of waste my friend. Our story at the beginning of this book (along with all these) hopefully will have you getting pretty bought-in regarding this WASTE premise ...and its potential costs.

**PEOPLE WASTE -** The Antithesis of Quality Leadership

## STUFF THAT HAPPENS BECAUSE RELATIONS ARE WEAK:

- Procrastinating on meeting with someone because you don't really like each other

- Don't tell my boss something because I'm unsure how he will receive it

- Don't share an idea because...

- Project meetings happening without all key players (cuz Joe is a pain in the butt and will slow us down)

- Meeting rescheduled (held again) when Joe finds out...

- Not having performance discussions

- Feedback not given or accepted because...

- Unresolved conflicts

- Take another route to get something done so I don't have to work with her

- Avoid socials and/or team-builders?!?

**JOURNALING - THOUGHTS GOING ON IN YOUR HEAD:**

_____
_____
_____
_____
_____
_____
_____
_____
_____
_____
_____
_____
_____

Day after day after day after day after day after day in the organizational-life ……….the waste goes on. A little bottlenecking here, a little there, a little all over the place. That's a LOT of 'littles' all over the place!

So instead of dealing with the real issue…

Companies spend 'zillions' of dollars on Quality Management programs (which isn't necessarily a bad thing mind you) to eliminate operational-waste. Yet we do essentially nothing to proactively and sustainably eliminate waste caused by poor communications, distrust, people dysfunction, ineffective leadership, and discomfort with other players, conversation-avoidance, etc.

## PEOPLE WASTE - The Antithesis of Quality Leadership

"...Yeah, it's an operational efficiency thing, right...! That'll fix all these jacked up relationships, behaviors and communication issues...."

We take on a 'major change' initiative with little to no foundation (leadership, communication, unresolved-people bottlenecks and relationships) in place. We (management) lie to ourselves, pretending 'we' the leadership and management are all good. "We got this LEADERSHIP and RELATIONSHIP piece, we're tight, all good, we got this..."

More waste, more wasted time...! Can you see the waste piling up yet?

You buying-in, accepting People Waste as a reality in YOUR world... YOUR sphere at least?

Are you ready to intentionally manage relations for optimal results ...throughout your sphere? You must first deal with YOU and your sphere. This can be mechanically managed by you first and then taught to others. This book is about how to do that, YOU ready?

- How about taking a moment right here and doing a quick assessment?
- Are you prepared to be transparent with yourself?

SO WE BEGIN.  For now generally think and picture your sphere (that world of people & players around you),

...your boss,

...all those you lead,

...your relationships with key players in all directions,

...team-mates, peers, leadership staff,

...those other (players) in other departments you have to (get to) work with,

...etc.

> So do you have that picture? The faces, names, and those people impacting your world - all of them?

<u>Let's jot down those names here (minimally capture all the ones you struggle with for now)!</u>

_____

_____

_____

**PEOPLE WASTE** - The Antithesis of Quality Leadership

_____
_____
_____
_____
_____
_____
_____
_____
_____
_____

Now think of all those relations you just wrote down in your sphere…. Now compare that group to an ideal utopian-scenario of a super-duper sphere of people and relations. Imagine this for a moment, as you think of perfect…

- perfect leadership in place (your boss, yours, your subordinate leaders)

- perfect relationships among ALL people (vertical, horizontal relations, internal/external relationships, relations with other departments, etc)

- perfect teamwork at your bosses level with his/her horizontal players

- perfect relationships, no knuckleheads anywhere
- always resolved conflicts and bottlenecks
- everyone within your sphere 'likes' each other making communications truly outstanding
- consensus occurs with all decisions and problem-solving
- synergy is big time happening!

> Okay, so we have that picture, right?

So if that 'utopian' or perfect picture of your sphere would be a '10 out of 10' - how do you rate your actual sphere of people and relationships? (Come on now, be real, honest with yourself, nobody is watching. It's just you and me here).

- Remember, that 'okay or just fine' is not a 10 …it is more like maybe a 6 or 7? Does that make sense?

So how do you rate your current sphere of relationships then? (10: high / 1: low)

> (    ?    ) out of 10

**PEOPLE WASTE -** The Antithesis of Quality Leadership

## JOURNALING - THOUGHTS GOING ON IN YOUR HEAD:

_____
_____
_____
_____
_____
_____
_____
_____
_____
_____
_____
_____
_____
_____
_____
_____
_____
_____
_____
_____

_____

Some brief explanation of 'waste-factoring',

For 'GRINS' let us say you placed a '<u>6.5</u>' in the space above. It could be a boss issue. It could be some of those reporting to you. Your team/peers? Some of your horizontals? Maybe other department players who you have to work with...

BTW, in simply me assessing leaders and students over the past decade or so - this initial snapshot self-assessing number is nearly always 'in the early stages' between 6.0 and 7.5   Just sayin'...

In working this proposed scenario of you saying you are a <u>6.5</u> (if that were the case) then that leftover <u>3.5</u> or 35% could be equated to as your waste (factor/impact). Unrealized potential.  'Fruit left on the vine' again comes to mind.

This is the waste going on in your spherical world of relationships!

Are you struggling with that <u>6.5</u>? If so, let's just say it's ONLY <u>2.5</u> or 25%.

You okay with ONLY 25% waste going on in your sphere of influence - simply due to your lack of managing your relationships?  Ouch.  That was kind of harsh huh?

**<u>JOURNALING - THOUGHTS GOING ON IN YOUR HEAD:</u>**

_____
_____
_____
_____

**PEOPLE WASTE -** The Antithesis of Quality Leadership

It is this author's belief that a real intentional focus on the *Leader's Relationship Sphere & your RVPs* can and will dramatically impact...

- productivity,
- bottom line profits,
- operational success,
- turnover,
- missed work time,
- happiness and job satisfaction,
- culture,
- future leadership recognition and professional success,
- that Synergy-thing,
- ultimately achieve results never before realized ….or even imagined.

Really?

Really!

**PEOPLE WASTE -** The Antithesis of Quality Leadership

OK, I'm pretty much done trying to sell you and convince you. This is all up to you. It is all on your shoulders my friend.

- ❖ This is your future leadership success here for the taking. It is time to begin truly MASTERING LEADERSHIP!

# 3

# RVP

*"Leadership is the capacity to translate vision into reality – to make it happen!"* Warren Bennis paraphrased

If people in your sphere are truly managed and nurtured and continuously focused upon – the vision we all really want likely will happen.

1) Relationships!

2) Conversations!

      …key to achieving Vision?

Yep!

**PEOPLE WASTE -** The Antithesis of Quality Leadership

<u>Moving on...</u> I am introducing a concept I have named and labeled Relational Value Points (RVP).

An RVP is a term for a (person) relationship in your sphere. RVPs are 'the people in your sphere'. An RVP requires attention, focus, effort, conversations, discussions, two-way accountability and actions executed on a consistent basis.

An example of an RVP would be Your Leader. He / she is one of your RVPs. He is that upward-vertical RVP, your boss. Like all RVPs, to be a '10' requires routinely-conducted real conversations, accountability, assessing, feedback, learning from each other, backing, reporting, updating, etc.

Within the pages ahead is a strategy and template for your execution to make your vision 'happen' ...utilizing RVPs. All of your RVPs! And yes again, even those OTHERS you struggle with off and on.

My 25 years of coaching/working with leaders, leadership, culture and organizational relationships has taught me 'this RVP template-strategy will work'. Implementing and executing this RVP concept is indeed about your Leadership Mastery my friend. When accomplished, you will be approaching the Epitome of Leadership Success!

Most anything else- any kind of shortcut or magic bullet effort will be a short-lived temporary fix by management (or you) - to unknowingly actually fix relationships. Some and maybe most people believe the biggest organizational challenge to be dealt with is communications.

It is in reality ...'relationships'!

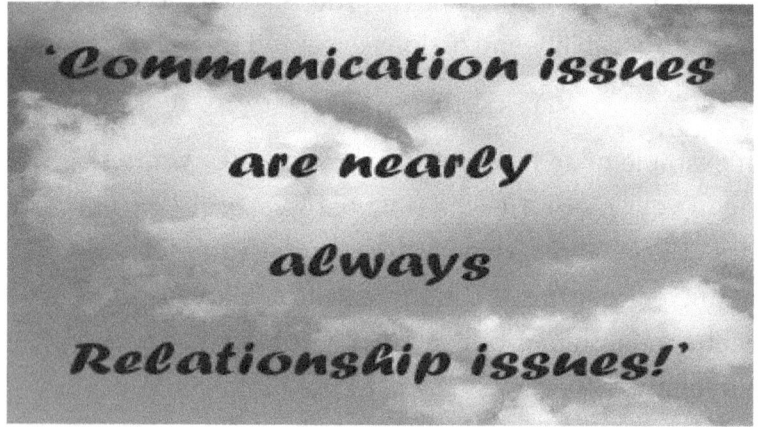

'Communication issues are nearly always Relationship issues!'

*NOTE*: Before moving on, I want you to know I gathered insight and feedback from the Human Resources community. I intentionally brought into this endeavor a few HR professionals to provide perspective and insight as well. There were various reasons why I wanted input from that side of the house.

**PEOPLE WASTE -** The Antithesis of Quality Leadership

One primary reasoning was that HR frequently experiences and suffers from this 'waste' premise. HR must waste their time as a result of ineffective managers and their dysfunctional relationships. Wow, that was also kind of harsh, wasn't it?

You see, they get dragged into 'wasting' their time on stuff because leaders didn't do their job! People, relations, communications, conflict resolution, culture and vision are a leader's leadership responsibility - not that of the HR office or manager.

See, there's that waste-thing raising its ugly head again!

I realized (in completing this book) a common message / theme exists within all my books. It is central to my overall beliefs about leadership development and people development in general. This message about relationship-building led me to writing this book and sharing it with you.

That central theme? Conversation. Dialogue. Feedback. It is the necessity of (for) 'never-ending-accountability-conversations' between people ...between RVPs. This relationship stuff requires effort; it does not just happen.

Relationship takes FTF / 1:1 conversations, discussions, consultations, confrontations, coachings and meetings routinely occurring to get there (to your vision). These 1:1's require transparency, courage and a commitment to listen and change behavior, by both parties. It takes your intentionality and persistence because we both know everyone won't be as interested in this as you are!

This simply means that if you and your sphere of players are going to improve through changed behavior, it will take targeted 'real' conversations. And this means more than one or two.

Lots of them – routinely occurring.

We all need accountability to change behavior in ourselves and others.

It is a two way street.

# 4

# ID YOUR SPHERE

*"What gets measured, gets done ...or improves at the very least"*

Tom Peters (paraphrased)

> Some quick review and further defining to share with you regarding the strategy and template.

### YOUR 'RELATIONSHIP SPHERE'

*Know it, own it'*

The well-known author Jim Collins spoke about 'getting the right people on the bus'. This is solid advice and wisdom; having the right players on your (bus) team is critical.

However, for our purpose here we are focusing on 'who is currently on the bus'. It is about controlling the 'controlables' that are on the bus! Getting different players onto the bus may be necessary - however in the beginning (right now), it is about working with who is on your bus right now. This is about ensuring strong relations with 'whoever is in those seats on our bus ...or sphere.'

The 'bus' in our lingo here (for remainder of book) will be referred to as your 'sphere'.

So who is in your sphere? We're getting there…

## **_RELATION VALUE POINT (RVP)_**

### *Know 'em, own 'em'*

Again, the RVP dynamic delves into the people, associations and connections that directly influence the success & happiness of the leader's world …your sphere.

The leader's actions have everything to do with your resulting culture (and achieved vision). The same holds true for the leader's sphere. The leader creates the culture, not vice versa. Many in management just find themselves settling into a culture, or sphere the way it is. Again, that's managing or maintaining. That's not us, not YOU! And you are not just going to exist within your sphere either, right?

Once more, a RVP is one of the key players within your (the leader's) sphere.

**PEOPLE WASTE -** The Antithesis of Quality Leadership

## ***RELATIONSHIP(S)***

### *Know 'em, own 'em*

A little 'definition' for our purposes here. Relationships (RVPs) = that functioning partnership between two people. Achieving this quality (the level I am suggesting here) of relationship with others may challenge you, and each of us - I get that. Many leaders struggle with personal / transparent relationship. This struggle limits the leader's success ...your success!

I also get and believe that 'real leadership' moves past this struggle; past that kind of 'limiting' thinking regarding relationships. It is about getting out of that shell of yours; past your insecurities; getting into knowing people and letting them know you!

DEFINING
Awesome leaders (like the ones you have thought of in reading this book) - people 'like' them; people 'feel' they care; people are allowed into their world; they are real, personable, open, transparent, etc!

A 10 out of 10 is our goal here with every RVP (player). Shouldn't it always be the goal? A functional relationship between two people (1:1) encompasses...

- Coaching / Feedback
- Workplace-functionality
- Supportive
- Accountability
- Problem-solving capability
- Professional Colleague
- Communication
- Always Accessible
- Transparency & Trust
- Mutual Development & Growth
- Friendship

Reminder from the opening paragraph of this book…

**PEOPLE WASTE -** The Antithesis of Quality Leadership

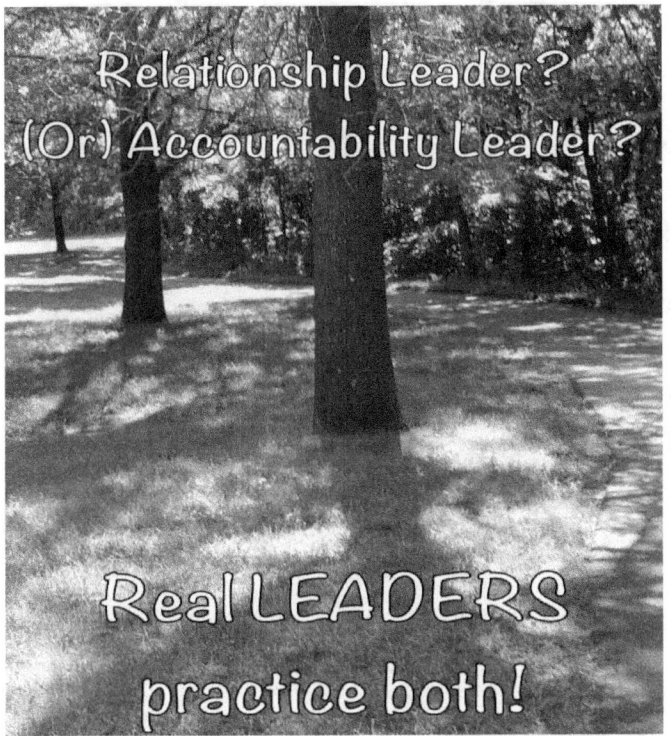

The REAL LEADER practices, understands and models both components of LEADERSHIP – 1) relationship and 2) accountability. This applies to each and every relationship (RVP) in your sphere. The quality RVP described would be about closeness in relationship and accountability regarding expectations, between both of you.

## LET'S GET BUSY. WORKING YOUR SPHERE...

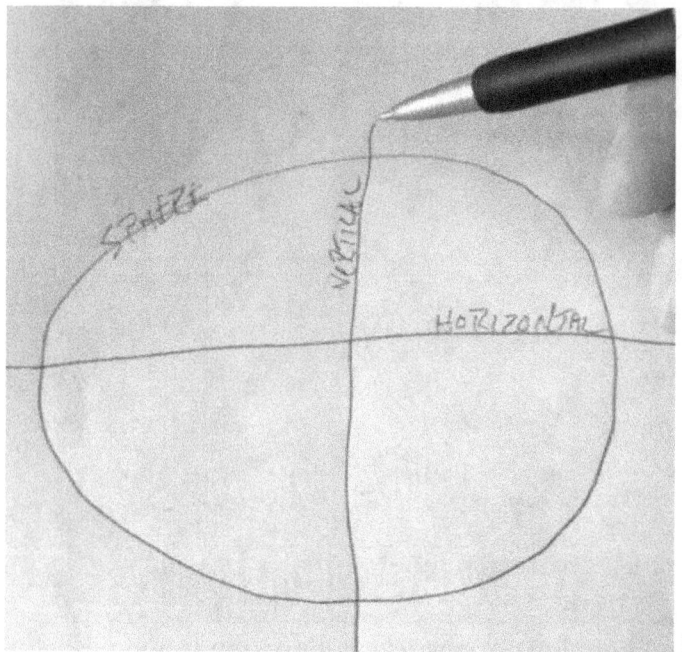

In its simplest form, think of your sphere as I have drawn in this image. To begin with, it is simply crossed lines – one horizontal line intersecting a vertical line.

---

Bonus information!!! *If you are one who struggles with remembering the difference between 'horizontal & vertical'... Try locking in on the 'horizon' which goes across the skyline from left to right (or east to west). See it out there? That's horizontal, the horizon, make sense? OK, you may not have needed that, but others may have; it's not all just about you, you know☺. OK, we move on now...*

**PEOPLE WASTE -** The Antithesis of Quality Leadership

That horizontal and vertical line intersection is the beginning of your world (sphere) of

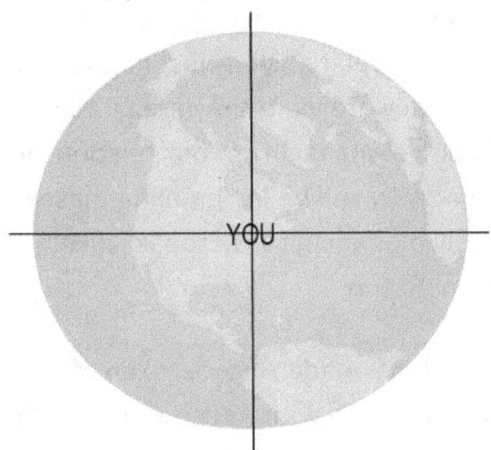

relationships...

Wherever you sit in an organization, you have players (people, relationships) instrumental to your success - in all directions. Simplified, there are those up & down (verticals) and those to your right & left (horizontals). *Before we finish, I will suggest some to you in a diagonal way as well☺.

These first few are likely your most obvious and critical RVPs upon which we focus. We need to understand these, see 'em, act on 'em, nurture 'em and own them.

Again many of us are just existing within our sphere - attempting to survive them (all these relationships) the way they are. Accepting them as they are...

Once again.... that's MANAGEMENT, maintaining!

Certainly it is not LEADERSHIP!

Once more, many in management passively let these critically key relationships just happen - some good, some not, but they are what they are…! Likely we have all done this 'passive' managing of our relationships. Many reading this right now will be 'resembling these remarks' and be passively managing as we speak …likely YOU may be there as you read this.

You may have made sincere token efforts to attempt a fix or address issues with RVPs …maybe. With no real concerted response or effort from the other party, we give up.

"I tried," we say to ourselves!

Come on you have done this and thought this…

Things are fixin' to change however! Leaders (like YOU☺) actively understand the relationship challenge and continue trying, nurturing them unceasingly …never endingly. Consider if all of us no longer accepted the insanity of 'bad' relationships day after day after day?

**PEOPLE WASTE -** The Antithesis of Quality Leadership

- Awareness is the first step to success here in regard to your sphere; do you see and understand who your players are?

- Just an FYI. I clearly didn't try to impress you with these graphics/pics. I intentionally left these drawings rough, to make a point – this is not some formal tool or drill; but a simple concept for any of us to quickly draw out and work on…(or for you to teach to others)!

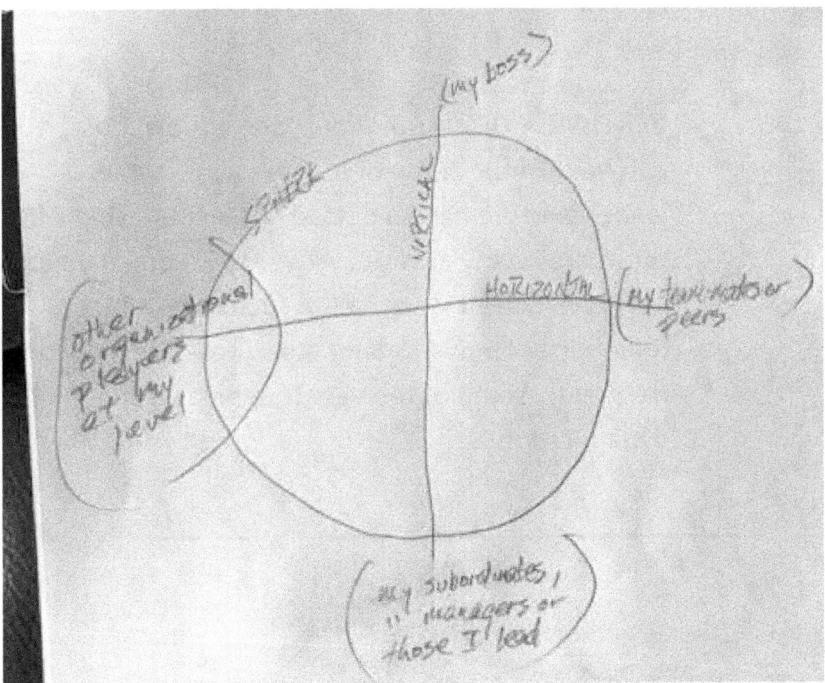

# ID YOUR SPHERE!

> Finally we are here. Execution time. Step One: Take a moment and put your sphere players (names) in the spaces below. For now leave the smaller space/blank to the right empty. Here we go...

**VERTICAL – UPWARD.** Your boss, your leader / vertical:

_____     _____


**VERTICAL – UPWARD.** (Your 'dotted-line' boss, IF you have one). Some of us have a secondary leader who we have a dotted line relationship with; these are nearly always awkward. Frequently non-profits / governments create such roles – board members, commissioners, etc. These are indeed frequently some of the very toughest relational dynamics for us:

_____     _____

**PEOPLE WASTE -** The Antithesis of Quality Leadership

◈ **VERTICAL(S) – DOWN.** Your subordinates or verticals; those employees or subordinate leaders (your team) reporting to you:

_____    _____

_____    _____

_____    _____

_____    _____

_____    _____

_____    _____

_____    _____

◈ **HORIZONTALS – YOUR TEAM.** Team-mates / peers (horizontals). These are your actual team-members that all report to your (same) boss:

_____    _____

_____    _____

_____   _____

_____   _____

_____   _____

_____   _____

◆ **HORIZONTALS – OUTSIDE YOUR TEAM.** Other organizational players (horizontal); these may not even be 'hierarchically' on your level. Maybe a bit above or below your level (depending on the dysfunction of your organization's structure).

These are all those that are not actually on your team but are to your left & right (horizontally), out there and over there... These are those people in other departments/areas (under other management). You need them (and they need you) for things to happen, for things to flow, and for things to work right. You may only work with them now and then, but they are part of making your world work – and vice versa!

*We typically uncover at least a couple of our trouble spots / problem folks for you s in this RVP-category. I'm betting you have a struggle with a few of the names you are getting ready to enter below (likely you don't even want to list them –

**PEOPLE WASTE** - The Antithesis of Quality Leadership

because you know what that will mean, don't you☺?) Yes, you have to list them – they are on your buss, your sphere:

_____      _____

_____      _____

_____      _____

_____      _____

_____      _____

_____      _____

_____      _____

_____      _____

_____      _____

# 5

# PROCESS PLANNING

*'Without Direction, We Wander'* (anonymous).

Mind you, this is NOT some short-term program to 'try' in your first 90 days, then to be abandoned! Rather this is a never-ending methodology of managing your Leadership - Relationship - World (sphere).

So this is your Plan of Attack – your 'Communications Ops Plan'.

Understanding all this, committing to it and then adapting it to your actual situation (your calendar and time-management tools) WILL get you where you want to be!

I did say WILL!

Really?

Really!

**PEOPLE WASTE -** The Antithesis of Quality Leadership

If intentionally executed along with selling it (modeling and subsequently teaching) constantly to your sphere of players, the vision WILL happen. It will then spread as people begin defining and working their spheres. It will all move to other leader's spheres as well. This can happen my friend.

### HUGELY COLOSSAL POINTS!

- All of this (RVP interactions) has to become as important as every other item on your agenda / on your calendar. It will become 'how you roll'.

- It is not about some 'stuff' to plug in IF you have time.

- It's not stuff to put on your calendar and then cancel or postpone.

- Realize that every time you cancel a people/relationship-building RVP conversation ...what's the message to that person?

**JOURNALING - THOUGHTS GOING ON IN YOUR HEAD:**

_____
_____
_____
_____
_____
_____
_____
_____
_____
_____
_____
_____
_____
_____
_____
_____
_____
_____
_____

You have to commit my friend. Because 'guess what I know that you also know?' You will ALWAYS have an excuse to NOT do people (RVP) stuff. Likely a pretty darned good excuse is always find-able. <u>You will NEVER have time for people, RVP-relationships and these needed conversations ...UNLESS YOU DO</u>!

**PEOPLE WASTE -** The Antithesis of Quality Leadership

Let's be real. If you are committed and it's on your calendar, it will get done. Chances are that it (RVP conversations) will happen if and only if you intentionally make it happen. If all this (RVP work) happens, so the vision will happen!

Trust the Coach on this and read on if you are still buying in... If you are committing to it?

This is a particularly mechanical, hard focus on your first 3-6 months of your leadership role. After that it will all still be necessary, but by then it will be a habit. And once you are seeing the fruits, the habit will have become a done deal. You will cease leaving grapes (waste) on the vine!

| Here are a couple of 'givens'... |
|---|

Assumption 1 - It's a given that you don't ever have to worry about finding time for all that 'business-operational stuff'. That's not ...NOT going to get scheduled and happen, right?

That's the stuff you and your company are all about – the product-making business or service you provide. You couldn't avoid spending necessary time on all that 'business-operational stuff' even if you wanted to, right?

Assumption 2 - It is also a given that you and I and every other manager has thought the thoughts going on in your head right now, "I'm sooooooo busy already, how do I plug more stuff into my calendar?
Or...I don't have time to talk to my whole sphere, those people, every month.
Or...It's too much confrontation.  Or...
I don't wanna"
Or...I gotta go do _____ (fill in the blank w/ something other than RVP conversations)"

Every *manager* worth his (or her) salt is busy, running crazy, going meeting to meeting, etc.  Any *manager* can do all that!  We all get that. This is all about the *leader* who intentionally focuses on specific behaviors, conversations and accountabilities related to RVPs - in order to achieve that Leadership Master thing.  And he/she also makes those other meetings as well☺.

Assumption 3 -- The great leaders we all know of, those one or two you have been picturing and thinking about... They ARE doing this relationship stuff ...this kind of intentional work! That's where you want to be, who you want to be like, right?

Assumption 4 – This will take self-discipline. You will indeed need to clear off your calendar a bit. You will need to begin delegating 'stuff' in all likelihood. You needed to do that anyway. Maybe you need to stop attending some of those easy, no-brainer, comfortable 'business-operational' meetings on your calendar anyway!

Many of those in actuality are only taking up your time
...because you don't trust him, her or them;
...because you are a micro-manager;
...because you didn't want to confront all this RVP-relational stuff;

...maybe you like having these excuses!??

- Noooooooooo....??! If you need some coaching and accountability help with this, give me a holler. I'm grinning at you by the way.
- Hey it's just you and me here. You still sticking with that story (those excuses)?

- ✓ This is for the leader who realizes it's no longer about just being the smartest one 'about' the industry or business.  <u>That is indeed what got you here, but not what will make you truly successful and happy going forward</u>.

- ✓ 'Trust the Coach' - this plan will take you to new heights.  Put these conversations and actions on your calendar and make each and every one happen – every day, every week, and month.

**PEOPLE WASTE -** The Antithesis of Quality Leadership

- ✓ Here is another truth I will just ask you to accept. That 'Peter Principle thing' we have all heard quoted, is really about leaders who never learned this RVP-learning here and therefore just managed (until their maintaining wasn't needed any longer).

They no longer lead (OR) manage... Peter is gone!

Really?

Really!

# 6

# VISIONING SUCCESS

*"Failure is the opportunity to begin again more intelligently."* Henry Ford

> I have been referencing Visioning success in one form or another in this book. This chapter does some 'connecting' of vision to spheres, RVPs, etc

## PICTURE THIS (ANOTHER STORY)

*YOU are in your first days on the job as the new Sr. Director for Operations at our company (from our story above - IMMC Inc and to create a scenario and clarify for our learning here)*

*Everything and everyone is new to you. You are in a brand new industry, in a brand new location, with all new people. Obviously that means all relationships are new as well. You with them, them with you, etc.*

*To this point, things have gone well and everyone is pretty happy. You have moved into some temporary lodging with your minimal belongings from the west coast, nearly 1100 miles away. Much of the family and friends are still back out west – a parent and two siblings & families. You are married with one kid but they won't be joining you for a few months to finish the school year. You are alone here, finding some friends will be important. That'll happen you figure, but for the moment you must focus on the job, what you were hired for...*

*You can worry about all that personal stuff after getting things under control and getting established here as 'the new sheriff in town' – at least within your department or market.*

*Anyway, around the office, things are a bit awkward as relationships are obviously in their initial stages, in all directions. However, it is that honeymoon phase which nearly always occurs in the initial days and even weeks. Everybody pretty much likes the new guy (you). It is all pretty wonderful actually. Good times ahead. There is new hope in the air. Conversations have a feeling of excitement as we begin anew. Lot of players met, lot more to meet and learn about; that'll happen sooner or later... You are hearing the usual stories of problem-people, other departments being issues, etc!*

*Yes, a honeymoon for most, except Jason who had hoped and pursued the position you were hired into; he's not a fan of yours now for sure. That part of things is definitely awkward; he'll come around. That will be a bit of a relationship challenge likely. It will work itself out you think to yourself. Everything and everyone will all be 'good' you sort of unconsciously accept as hours and days get to rolling behind you.*

*Seems like a good bunch of people more or less; clearly a few misfits. One jerk for sure over there in the Contracted Services/Vendors office. There are always a few it seems.*

*You call a meeting for Friday of your third week. You are thinking it's time to take the next step which all your management learning has taught you – let's do some VISIONING!*

*Been there done that, you've led these visioning talks before...*

*So you gather your five guys (management staff) – four males and one female (all managers in title) to do some brainstorming. After some introductory comments, conversation and theorizing about visioning – you begin. You start some questioning,*

*"We need a vision to work towards...*

*Where are we trying to take this department?*

*What would it look like if we achieved it...?*

*Of course we must make good products, we want to be the best-of-the-best, great quality products and all that; but let's focus on the people-piece right now...*

*I want this to be a great market and team. What is a great* market or team anyway? What would it look like and feel like if we created one?

So anyway, let's put some words on the board to just get a feel for where we want to take this team in the near future...

Where do we want to be in six months, a year or so down the road?

What is our vision guys?"

[*The words begin to flow as you and your green dry erase marker capture them*]:

■■■■■■■■■■■■■■■■■■■■■■■■■■■■■■■■■■■■■■■■■■■■■■■

- Family feeling
- Supportive
- Good relationships
- Open Communications
- Trust
- Respect
- Transparency

- Solve problems together
- Care about one another
- Collaborative
- Loyalty to the Absent
- Great Results
- Fun
- Problem solvers
- People are empowered…

Some brief discussions occur periodically during the brainstorming. There was a bit of the usual bad-mouthing and attitudes expressed about a few of the players within the warehouse and customer service departments. Hard to believe nobody mentioned the jerk in the Vendors office.

Again, all nod and confirm to each other "…there's always a few bad apples huh?" We'll work through all that, and those you assure them. We'll get 'em on the team!

This is working, this was a good exercise you think. Good start.

*In fact, it is a good thing being attempted right?*

**PEOPLE WASTE -** The Antithesis of Quality Leadership

Time to begin wrapping up, "OK, that's cool. I like it, so that's our goal or vision; let's make this happen. This will be about us, and it's up to the six of us, this leadership team, to make it (vision) become our reality. Let's keep talking about this. Good stuff really, I appreciate the thinking, the energy and what we have here gang. Matt, can you make some kind of visual thing with these words, etc and put a couple up around the office? Put them in a nice frame maybe? This will help with awareness, reminding us, focus us and help us be accountable to each other in going after this vision."

Some chit chat follows, cut off by you after a few minutes, "OK, again good job gang. Now get back to work!" You say this of course jokingly as everyone gathers their stuff to get back to reality – our jobs, problems, and business as usual.

You know, the real work here – doing Injection Molding, procurement issues, business needs to pick up, talking about people, customer service, sales, belly aching about knucklehead, the new quality control dynamics – all that normal business stuff!

- If you have been down this road a few times, then you know that indeed ALL will be back to business totally within a few days or a week at most. Good talk though, good stuff to spend a few minutes on; good management stuff. That's how these things work... Feels good.

As you head back to your office smiling, you are thinking, "we're off and running toward that vision that 'we' created. Good start. This visioning-stuff works, good exercise, a little relationship building just occurred in there as well. Jason was even pretty well involved, he'll come around I'm sure. Need a warm up of my coffee and call the boss to fill him in...."

- What's happened?

- What's changed?

- What is going to happen from here?

- You been there, done that (this)?

**PEOPLE WASTE -** The Antithesis of Quality Leadership

**JOURNALING - THOUGHTS GOING ON IN YOUR HEAD:**

_____
_____
_____
_____
_____
_____
_____
_____
_____
_____
_____
_____
_____
_____
_____
_____
_____
_____

- We've all seen these kinds of management tips and strategies used; maybe you have even facilitated such an exercise. Maybe we will get there, maybe not. Was a plan put into place or did we just envision a vision?

- Are there specific intentional actions you ought to take to make this vision happen?

- Now go back a few pages and ponder that list of vision-words. Were they good words? Spend a few moments here. Really, what would have to happen by you and others to make those words become reality (our vision)? What will be the challenge(s) of making it all happen?

**<u>JOURNALING - THOUGHTS GOING ON IN YOUR HEAD</u>:**

## PEOPLE WASTE - The Antithesis of Quality Leadership

I am here suggesting that more often than not, this well-intended effort slowly fades - as do the words and graphics on the nicely framed wall hangings! You know that one outside the manager's door and the other one at the department exit. Again no lack of good intention exists here, it's just stuff and conversation that gets easily shoved to the back burner by all that Injection-Molding biz stuff which we must get done.

Likely it (the vision) will now and then resurface or be mentioned….

- It will remain 'out there' as 'that vision' where we are hoping to go. What will also remain *out there* is 'the plan or strategy to execute'. Achieving it or not may not really ever even come up again for some number of months …years!?!

*What we need here is a plan, or maybe even a template! Just assuming the vision just described will just happen is well, just flawed thinking!*

# 7

# NOW ASSESS YOUR SPHERE

*"Effective Leaders realize you must get the Heart before asking for the Hand."* anonymous

### BACK TO YOUR REAL WORLD (SPHERE)

You identified your RVPs (back in Chapter 4). Think through this for a bit, did you get them all (RVPs) captured / written down? Here are some questions to ask of yourself as you ponder all this:

- Who has influence or involvement in my results / success?
- Who all impacts how I get things done?
- Who needs me?
- Who do I need?
- Who could help me?
- Those problem departments?
- Who has an impact on my downline's productivity and/or success ...or happiness?

**PEOPLE WASTE -** The Antithesis of Quality Leadership

> Now begins our next step. Do an initial assessment of your sphere/players. Go back to the names you inserted (Chapter 4) when we ID'd your sphere. But wait, read through this below before you do the rating...

Next to each player's name was a smaller blank to the right. With each name listed, do an initial rating of your RELATIONSHIP with each one. But wait, first...

Before doing so, consider the three pieces of information below:

- ❖ Consider a '10' as an absolutely solid tremendous relationship. Consequently a '1' is a really bad relationship. As you think of a '10' relationship, consider the list of relationship factors we presented a few pages back on p. 79.

- ❖ <u>This is NOT an assessment of '**how you think they do their job'**</u>. This is NOT you evaluating their performance. This IS about how you rate YOUR RELATIONSHIP with each of them! The number (1-10) is about the quality of the relationship (not their work/performance as a ….). Obviously their performance of duties may impact the relationship, but the focus here is on the RVP and your relationship with him/her.

- ❖ I would also suggest that even if the 'relationship' is good but you do not connect enough to know them very well, that makes your rating low (bad). This therefore would suggest that someone who is brand new to the organization (or you are new to someone) and sitting within your sphere automatically gets a subpar rating simply because you do not know each other!

**PEOPLE WASTE -** The Antithesis of Quality Leadership

- ❖ It's at least to some degree a temporary bottleneck, right?

- ❖ OK, one last very important point about all this. <u>'Bad' is not to mean necessarily that the person is bad. It's not about a bad person - but the relationship is bad.</u> Ponder that, you need to get this before you go practicing or teaching it after all.

---

OKAY NOW GO AHEAD... Go back to your list and rate each of them. Do it now and be real, and be honest. It is only the two of us here - no one is seeing how you rate each, for now anyway.

> *As iron sharpens iron,*
> *so a friend sharpens a friend.*
>
> PROVERBS 27:17

**Done? OK. So as you look back at each of your RVPs and the rating you gave each...**

**PEOPLE WASTE** - The Antithesis of Quality Leadership

## What are your thoughts? **?**

- ⊕ Regarding your relationships in general?
- ⊕ Regarding 'people waste'?
- ⊕ Regarding your success and productivity?
- ⊕ Regarding 'continuous improvement' of each RVP (getting worse, getting better)?
- ⊕ Regarding your downline/subordinates; how are they impacted by your 'bad' up-above-them horizontal RVPs?
- ⊕ Regarding the impact of those sphere-relations on your results, happiness, productivity, making money, etc?
- ⊕ Regarding that overall rating # you gave to your sphere earlier; what was it? (_____) Do you need to change it? I'm betting by going through this exercise, through each of these individual RVPs – your overall assessment (#) has changed.
- ⊕ How are you thinking of that original assessment way back there where you were thinking of things as being FINE, OK, NO BIGGEE, ALL GOOD, etc?

## **JOURNALING - THOUGHTS GOING ON IN YOUR HEAD:**

# 8

# YOUR OTHER RVP(s)

*"A genuine leader is not a searcher for consensus but a molder of consensus."* Martin Luther King

---

**BUT WAIT, THERE'S MORE!   MORE RVP's...!**

---

We're going a bit deeper here now regarding your life and sphere.

The RVPs you named and have now assessed are clearly your most obvious RVPs within your sphere.  However there are other players who impact you and make your world better or worse.  They are also crucial to your overall success, happiness and future.

Realize this.  In a few cases the (RVPs) I am proposing below - you may not even have someone in that particular part of your life or sphere.

However I am suggesting and it is my belief that these are necessary and/or important relationships (measurements) in your world or sphere.

*Again, leaders manage their world.
Their world doesn't manage them.*

Here are the rest of your other RVPs (according to Booker anyway).

<u>CONSIDER</u>:

- ❖ If there is no one (or nothing) to go in the blank as you work on these below, the rating is obviously a '0'!

- ❖ As you will see, some of these are very personal to you and therefore you may not even see the need. Obviously this is your choice. I'm just sayin' and suggestin' ….these should be on your calendar and be given their due diligence. They should be managed and focused upon as well as the rest.

> ✓ Here are some other RVPs which should possibly be intentionally managed as well. As you place names here, go ahead and do an initial rating as well…

**PEOPLE WASTE -** The Antithesis of Quality Leadership

Your **SIGNIFICANT OTHER** or family connection. This family piece (RVP) is hugely significant to your world and when absent or 'bad' leaves us out of balance. Maybe we call this your 'personal family support structure RVP'. Maybe you are currently without one or maybe it is just 'not good' at the moment. Might be a missing RVP in your life. ☹ - That's a '0' for the moment.

_____     _____

_____     _____

**FAMILY or FRIENDSHIPS.** Family issues going on or maybe all is very good with immediate family players? Additionally this may be a place to assess your friendships – enough friends? In good shape? Need some maintenance? Only you know my friend. We need friendship; seems to me this could be family or not...

_____     _____

_____     _____

_____     _____

_____   _____

_____   _____


- **MENTOR or ADVISOR inside** (someone or maybe a couple of players, senior managers or execs above you) – *in your organization* - someone to help you with personal / professional growth.  This could obviously be for future help as well in helping you improve now, move upward and onward (if that's your desire).

_____   _____

_____   _____


- **MENTOR or COACH outside** (someone or maybe a couple of respected players/leaders or maybe an actual professional 'Leadership/Exec Coach') - outside the organization.

_____   _____

- **COMMUNITY RELATIONS** (this is smart on many levels - to be connected within the community to some quality people). May help you with growing your business; or maybe someone to help you find a job someday; or maybe someone you can help. Connections and quality relationships are priceless.

    *In my coaching with leaders, I advise them to be adding 'one quality person to your world' every month! If you don't really have any or maybe just not enough, mark it lower appropriately. Begin adding these to your world.

    _____        _____

    _____        _____

    _____        _____

    _____        _____

    _____        _____

- **MY CULTURE, the one I lead.** This may seem strange, but I encourage you to think of that

Culture you vision-ed (the one you are trying to create) as another of your sphere relations... It is a RVP itself. Ponder that for a moment.

*The point here is to keep the awareness and focus on that culture (RVP) and how it is developing or not? Monthly place it on your calendar to talk to others about, think about, assess, do a management brainstorming, grow it, etc. Are you tracking well in terms of achieving that vision?

_____*Culture*_____  _____

<sub>RVP</sub> **GOD**. For me, I clearly would have a RVP (of my relationship with my God). Maybe depending on how you roll – this is your spiritual connection or that faith piece or that entity that brings you peace...?!?

_____  _____

## PEOPLE WASTE - The Antithesis of Quality Leadership

- **HEALTH / FITNESS.** For me, this is a must RVP as well. This is one of my RVPs just to ensure I am keeping tabs on my health, fitness, mental well-being, time to self, reading, financial health, etc. This is about taking care of your mind, body and future. This may include working out, listening to music, a hobby, personal business stuff, a passion, community involvement or whatever makes you ROLL & GO. Find time for YOU and your stuff!

  _____  _____

- **THINKING TIME.** Yes, time to just think. Time to just sit preferably earlier in the day, during business hours. The door is shut, I am here for ME, to think – how am I doing? [Maybe it is just that time where you do *this* assessment once/month; think about it and plan out the next month's calendar].

  _____  _____

**_ANY OTHER RVPs?_** (Plz ponder this a bit, maybe there is another dynamic of your life worth intentionally monitoring and measuring in such a way!)

RVP _____  _____

RVP _____  _____

RVP _____  _____

RVP _____  _____

RVP _____  _____

# 9

# MAKING IT HAPPEN

*"Coming together is a beginning, keeping together is progress, and working together is success."* Henry Ford

---

| The RVP Process simply put, looks like this: |
|---|

1. Commit to continuously improving your relationships

2. Identify Who? ….your sphere of players (RVPs)

3. Rate those RVPs

4. Schedule (invites on your calendar) each RVP for next month's conversations

5. After initial meetings and getting their buy-in, both you and the RVP should do a rating of each other before you walk into the conversation every month

6. Conduct conversations (assess - do gap analysis of differences of how you each rated it - where we go from here - commit to continuing – how we improve the process…)

7. Work on RVPs in between conversations (daily interactions, accountabilities in place, etc)

8. Involve others to help with perspective and accountability

9. <u>*Repeat sequence every month… Every month, every RVP!*</u>

The approach, courage required and challenge of some of these RVP conversations is not spoken to in great detail in this book. Truly some of these RVPs could be tough to deal with; find help with this if need be but do not avoid. The benefits will always outweigh the inconvenience and difficulty of conversation. Feel free to call me; I am happy to help. Remember it's all just about CONTINUOUS IMPROVEMENT OF RELATIONSHIPS and…

*'Failure is not an Option'* Apollo 13 movie

The bottom line and message for you here is <u>'begin to manage it'!</u> Cease allowing your sphere (of players) to manage you!

This book was to create awareness, get your attention, give you some tools, sell you on the need and initiate a beginning! Please start leading your relationships and start eliminating People Waste ...at least within YOUR sphere!

### *The Principles & Practices of*
# SIGNIFICANCE

- Peace
- Transparent
- Forgiving
- Love / Relationship
- Learner
- Service
- Thankful
- Fruitful

*"How we live our life matters!"*

(From my book SIGNIFICANCE Starts Now – How We Live Our Lives Matters)

A few last tips & hints as you launch your Leadership Mastery (and not becoming a 'Peter')!

Be aware of these and be prepared as you jump into challenging communications and your new way of doing business...

- Be conscious (even if you are sold here) when you reach out to 'certain players', he/she may not be so agreeable. Realize they didn't read the book! Commit, persist, seek their buy-in and make it happen! Give them a copy of the book☺.

- In one of the first few conversations, consider sharing your whole sphere-thinking and allow them to understand he/she is one of the important players in your sphere! Stroking their ego 'as important' could be a great way of beginning things.

- Ask others how they see your relationships - get other perspective which in turn triggers more quality relationship-building conversations. Think about it.

- Over time, as you really begin 'living it' and working it - share concepts and your practices with others. That's a good thing – teaching; teach it up, down and sideways!

- A last tip I would share whenever you approach difficult conversations, conflicts and confrontational meetings... Capture in writing carefully all you really want to say beforehand. During meeting give them a copy as well, this will force you to deal with 'everything' intended. Otherwise things may come out wrong or not be said. Listen to the Coach on this one my friend.

**PEOPLE WASTE -** The Antithesis of Quality Leadership

## January

| Sunday | Monday | Tuesday | Wednesday | Thursday | Friday | Saturday |
|---|---|---|---|---|---|---|
|  |  |  |  | 1 | 2 | 3 |
| 4 | 5 | 6 | 7 | 8 | 9 | 10 |
| 11 | 12 | 13 | 14 | 15 | 16 | 17 |
| 18 | 19 | 20 | 21 | 22 | 23 | 24 |
| 25 | 26 | 27 | 28 | 29 | 30 | 31 |

February...!

April...!

May...!

June...!

July...!

August...!

Sept...!

Oct...!

Nov...!

December...!

*(Do you realize how much better, accurate & easier the Annual Performance Process will now be since you did these monthly talks!)*

Jan...!

Feb...!

March........

## *OK, you get it, right?!?*

# 10

# WRAPPING 'ER UP

*"Most people in general and management specifically believe 'communicating' to be the biggest organizational challenge. In fact it is not. The reality is that 'relationships' is nearly always the actual challenge and root-cause problem."* ME☺

Relationships can be 'bad' or 'good' or even ugly - that's a matter of choice. Real leaders realize they can develop a good relationship with anyone if they choose to (and yes, whether the other person is committed or not).

Accepting a bad relationship and living with it 'day after day after day' is insanity. This is how maintain-ers and followers exist. Employees and followers can get away with this kind of existence; leaders don't get to play these petty games. Many do still.

Allowing ineffective relationships is not leading - that's managing ...that's maintaining. Building, fixing, understanding and nurturing relations is the leader's job ...and that's leadership. This is all also culture-building (which leaders are responsible to do on top of everything else).

This book's message was all obviously about improving

one's leadership-sphere and work-world.  <u>Maybe not so obvious is the how this improves one's quality of life as well!</u>

## *'Bad' relationships = People Waste!*

For the high performing and up-to-this-point successful senior leader – this all will determine their future year's successes (or not).  You will *succeed colossally* or this will be your *stumbling block* - if not grasped, realized and intentionally addressed.  I will furthermore point out, even if you are achieving pretty solid results within your verticals (relationships), you had better be nurturing those horizontals!

That's Leadership my friend.

Many a leader has moved rapidly up into near-the-top management roles only to realize the other senior leaders (peers) are really 'now' the key to their future success.  Having never learned how to do this effectively leaves many senior managers and execs with a serious flat-spot.  Trust the Coach, this can and does happen.  Due to this, many C-suite Exec teams are literally among the worst teams in the organization.

**PEOPLE WASTE** - The Antithesis of Quality Leadership

Wherever you sit or do your leadership thing – 'relationships' is absolutely the key to getting where you want to go.

As I will nearly always leave leaders with, here's my favorite leadership quote:

> *"People don't care how much you know until first they know how much you care."*

Believe me when I tell you this quote's meaning totally applies to not just your leadership success but just as much to your relationship success. Digest this. Get this!

A few last repeated and reinforcing points:

- Relationships will be the key to your ultimate success at work and at life!

- Relationships is not politics, it is your job!

- You need people all around you to help you succeed! Realize those 'others' see you as an 'other'...

- You (the leader) are accountable for achieving the Vision! A strategy is required; the vision wall-hanger on its own, won't do it.

- What we put on our calendar - happens! Include RVP conversations routinely.

- Leadership is not just knowing & managing the business stuff. It is at the very least, 50% about people stuff!

- "….Managers maintain (the way things are). Leaders build, improve, make things happen and grow (themselves and others)…"


Take good care my friend, and take care of yours!

Doug

**PEOPLE WASTE -** The Antithesis of Quality Leadership

# WHEN LEADERS CHANGE
## so then do
# ORGANIZATIONS, CULTURES & TEAMS

Douglas M. Booker

# SUPPLEMENTAL REFERENCES:

*...writings on the costs of 'bad' <u>organizational relationships and people issues</u>...*

> NOTE: Although it was never my intention to provide proof, research and/or evidence regarding the validity of the concepts in this book - I chose to provide some links! These are not intended to be academic citations, but rather simply 'googling topics' I used where I found interesting information relevant to our topics here.

- *Stressful Workplace Relationships*
- *10 Signs your Workplace is Toxic*
- The Dysfunctional Workplace
- The Bottom Line Impact of People Problems in the Workplace
- Scholarly Articles, Impact of People Behaviors in Workplace
- Organizational Behavior
- Culture and People challenges
- Negative Behaviors in the Workplace
- The Real Cost of Workplace Conflict
- Management relationships
- Silos and Organizational Communications
- Leadership and Accountability

Douglas M. Booker

# AUTHOR / BOOKS

(BIOGRAPHY))

President and Founder of Booker Training Associates; Doug is a Facilitator, Change Agent, Coach, Author & Leadership-Developer. Booker Training Associates is a business Doug began after a successful military career and early-retiring as a Major from the Army in 1992. The idea for his work evolved as Doug began realizing the 'challenge' facing individuals and organizations in managing people with un-developed leadership.

Ultimately he focuses on leadership behavior - helping not just the leader or manager, but organizationally with what he calls their 'People-Systems'.

A strong believer in the need for continued learning, he has completed many certifications along with earning a Master's degree in Management. In his 25 years of serving organizations and individual leaders, Doug has worked with various industries concentrating on Leadership growth and Cultural improvement. He also teaches in Higher Education with various universities. Along with his teaching and consulting work, he has now authored eight books - five books on Leadership; one on personal growth titled 'SIGNIFICANCE Starts Now'; a short Biographical Novel; and one which he refers to as his little God book 'Triangles, Compasses & GOD'.

Doug regards his wife Sydney, two children, siblings and extended family as the best parts of his life. A close 2nd is being able to work in a field that he loves – teaching and helping people in need (a ministry of sorts).

Doug was selected as the Army's National Leadership Trainer/Professor of the Year in 1989; receiving this recognition from the Secretary of Defense in Washington D.C. He was also recently distinguished as Faculty of the Year at a local university where he part-time teaches.

Doug's favorite quote, which he asks people to hold him accountable to practice in life and work:

*"People don't care how much you know, until they first know how much you care."*

**PEOPLE WASTE -** The Antithesis of Quality Leadership

www.bookertraining.com
913.232.0244

5020 Indian Creek Pkwy, Overland Park, KS 66207

**Linked In & Facebook** (Doug Booker), **Twitter** (DouglasMBooker)

doug@bookertraining.com

*"I would love to hear from you regarding this book or any of my other books as well. Always open for a talk about 'Leadership, Faith, People, Culture, Relationships, etc. I always enjoy adding new quality people to my life; so let's talk!"*

Douglas M. Booker

**PEOPLE WASTE -** The Antithesis of Quality Leadership

## Previous books:

## *Teaching Fishing for Managers,* 2009

## *Leadership Conversations - Rebuilding on Rock*, 2010

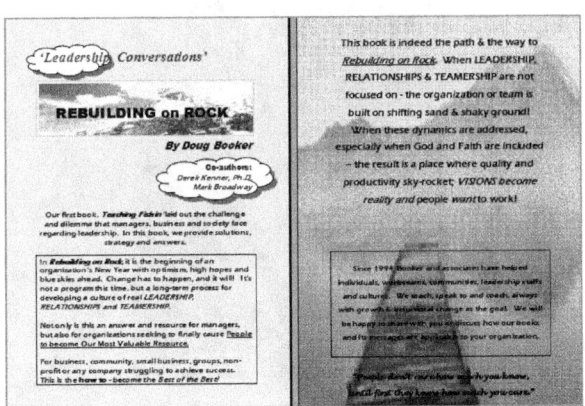

***The Conference for Leaders***, 2011

***SIGNIFICANCE Starts Now – How We Live Our Lives Matters***, 2012

## TRIANGLES, COMPASSES & GOD, 2013

## 'KNOWINGLY LEADING - 25 Conversations to Success' 2014

www.ingramcontent.com/pod-product-compliance
Lightning Source LLC
Chambersburg PA
CBHW070259190526
45169CB00001B/477